Collins

TREASURE HOUSE

Pupil Spelling Skills

Author: Sarah Snashall

HarperCollins Publishers
Since 1817

William Collins' dream of knowledge for all began with the publication of his first book in 1819.

A self-educated mill worker, he not only enriched millions of lives, but also founded a flourishing publishing house. Today, staying true to this spirit, Collins books are packed with inspiration, innovation and practical expertise. They place you at the centre of a world of possibility and give you exactly what you need to explore it.

Collins. Freedom to teach.

Published by Collins
An imprint of HarperCollins*Publishers*
The News Building
1 London Bridge Street
London
SE1 9GF

Browse the complete Collins catalogue at
www.collins.co.uk

© HarperCollins*Publishers* Limited 2017

10 9 8 7 6 5 4 3 2 1

ISBN 978-0-00-823652-6

All rights reserved. No part of this publication may be reproduced, stored in a retrieval system, or transmitted in any form or by any means, electronic, mechanical, photocopying, recording or otherwise, without the prior written permission of the Publisher or a licence permitting restricted copying in the United Kingdom issued by the Copyright Licensing Agency Ltd., 90 Tottenham Court Road, London W1T 4LP.

British Library Cataloguing in Publication Data
A Catalogue record for this publication is available from the British Library

MIX
Paper from responsible sources
FSC www.fsc.org **FSC C007454**

FSC™ is a non-profit international organisation established to promote the responsible management of the world's forests. Products carrying the FSC label are independently certified to assure consumers that they come from forests that are managed to meet the social, economic and ecological needs of present and future generations, and other controlled sources.

Find out more about HarperCollins and the environment at
www.harpercollins.co.uk/green

Publishing Director: Lee Newman
Publishing Manager: Helen Doran
Senior Editor: Hannah Dove
Project Manager: Emily Hooton
Author: Sarah Snashall
Development Editor: Jessica Marshall
Copy-editor: Gaynor Spry
Proofreader: Tanya Solomons
Cover design and artwork: Amparo Barrera and Ken Vail Graphic Design
Internal design concept: Amparo Barrera
Typesetter: Jouve India Private Ltd
Illustrations: Leesh Li (Beehive illustration), Beatriz Castro, Aptara and QBS
Production Controller: Rachel Weaver

Printed and bound by Grafica Veneta SpA

Contents

	Page
Unit A: Spelling /ai/	4
Unit B: Spelling /ee/	6
Unit C: Spelling /igh/	8
Unit D: Spelling /oa/	10
Unit E: Spelling /oo/	12
Unit F: Spelling /oi/	14
Unit G: Spelling /ar/	16
Unit H: Spelling the /e/ sound ea	18
Unit I: Spelling /ur/	20
Unit J: Spelling the short /oo/	22
Unit K: Spelling /or/	24
Review unit 1	26
Unit L: Spelling /ou/	28
Unit M: Spelling /air/	30
Unit N: Spelling /ear/	32
Unit 1: Spelling –ff, –ll, –ss and –zz	34
Unit 2: Spelling –ck after a short vowel	36
Unit 3: Spelling –nk	38
Unit 4: Spelling words with two syllables	40
Unit 5: Spelling the /ch/ sound tch	42
Unit 6: Spelling words that end in a /v/ sound	44
Unit 7: Adding –s	46
Unit 8: Adding –es to make a plural	48
Review unit 2	50
Unit 9: Adding –ing to a root word	52
Unit 10: Adding –er to a root word	54
Unit 11: Adding –ed to a root word	56
Unit 12: Adding –er and –est to adjectives	58
Unit 13: Spelling words ending in –y	60
Unit 14: Spelling ph	62
Unit 15: Spelling wh	64
Unit 16: Spelling words with k	66
Unit 17: Adding the prefix un–	68
Unit 18: Spelling compound words	70
Unit 19: Spelling the days of the week	72
Unit 20: Spelling common exception words	74
Review unit 3	76

Spelling Unit A

Spelling /ai/

The long **/ai/** sound can be spelt:

ai as in gr**ai**n, st**ai**n and p**ai**nt

–ay as in pl**ay**, st**ay** and m**ay**

a–e as in pl**ate**, c**ake** and g**ale**

When the long **/ai/** sound comes at the end of a word, use the **–ay** spelling.

Get started

Sort these words into those with a short **/a/** sound (as in **pat**) and words with a long **/ai/** sound (as in **plate**). Put the words into a table like the one below. One has been done for you.

1. map
2. maid
3. man
4. made
5. mash
6. mate
7. main
8. mat
9. may
10. mad

Short /a/ as in pat	Long /ai/ as in plate
map	

Try these

Copy and complete these words with **a–e**, **ai** or **–ay**. Remember, the **–ay** spelling is only used at the ends of words. One has been done for you.

1.  t r _ _ n

   Answer: *train*

2.  g _ t _

3.  p l _ _

4.  w h _ l _

5.  h _ _

6.  r _ _ n

Now try these

Copy each sentence. Choose the right spelling for the missing word. One has been done for you.

1. Put the cups on the _____.   (tray / trai)

   Answer: *Put the cups on the tray.*

2. _____ for me, Jacob!   (Wait / Wate / Wayt)

3. We went to the _____ to swim.   (laik / lake / layk)

4. Don't be _____, Trish.   (afraid / afrade / afayd)

5. You can _____ a cake.   (taik / take / tayk)

6. Which _____ shall we go?   (wai / way)

Spelling Unit B

Spelling /ee/

The most common ways to spell the long **/ee/** sound are:

ee as in b**ee**, thr**ee** and sn**ee**ze

ea as in **ea**t, b**ea**t and tr**ea**t

Get started

Sort these words into those with a short **/e/** sound (as in **set**) and words with a long **/ee/** sound (as in **sleep**). Put the words into a table like the one below. One has been done for you.

1. bee
2. beep
3. bet
4. beam
5. bent
6. beach
7. bleach
8. bend
9. bead
10. bed

Short **/e/** as in **set**	Long **/ee/** as in **sleep**
	bee

Try these

Copy and complete these words with **ee** or **ea**. One has been done for you.

1. f _ _ t

    Answer: *feet*

2. l _ _ f

3. t _ _ t h

4. c o f f _ _

5. t _ _ c h e r

6. t r _ _

Now try these

Copy each sentence. Choose the right spelling for the missing word. One has been done for you.

1. You can _____ in here.   (squeeze / squeaze)

    Answer: *You can squeeze in here.*

2. Say '_____'!   (pleese / please)

3. Suki was sick last _____.   (week / weak)

4. My coat is _____.   (green / grean)

5. Max and Toby are on the same _____.   (teem / team)

6. Don't _____ with your mouth full! (speek / speak)

Spelling Unit C

Spelling /igh/

The most common ways to spell the long **/igh/** sound are:

igh as in l**igh**t, br**igh**t and s**igh**

i–e as in sh**ine**, p**ine** and f**ile**

–y as in fl**y**, sh**y** and cr**y**

Get started

Sort these words into those with a short **/i/** sound (as in **bit**) and words with a long **/igh/** sound (as in **bright**). Put the words into a table like the one below. One has been done for you.

1. sigh
2. sight
3. sit
4. shine
5. sink
6. slide
7. slight
8. sing
9. spine
10. sly

Short **/i/** as in **bit**	Long **/igh/** as in **bright**
	sigh

Try these

Copy and complete these words with **igh**, **i–e** or **–y**. One has been done for you.

1. b r _ d _

    Answer: bride

2. b _ k _

3. l _ _ _ t

4. s t r _ p _ s

5. n _ _ _ t

6. f l _

Now try these

Copy each sentence. Choose the right spelling for the missing word. One has been done for you.

1. Can you _____ me to school?
   (drighve / drive / dryve)

   Answer: Can you drive me to school?

2. Ouch! These shoes are too _____. (tight / tite / tyte)

3. What is the _____? (tighm / time / tyme)

4. Please don't _____. (crigh / crie / cry)

5. Tina and Dad made a camp _____.
   (fighr / fire / fyre)

6. You gave me a _____! (fright / frite / fryt)

9

Spelling Unit D

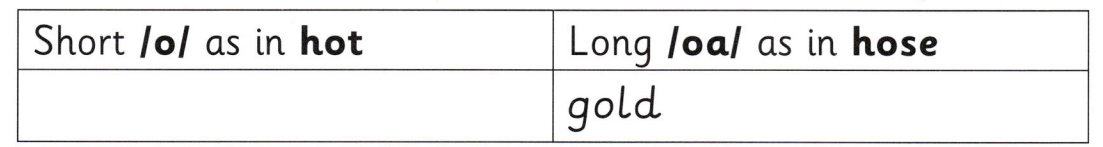

Spelling /oa/

The most common ways to spell the long **/oa/** sound are:

oa as in t**oa**d, fl**oa**t and f**oa**m

o–e as in h**o**m**e**, st**o**n**e** and w**o**k**e**

ow as in sn**ow**, b**ow** and arr**ow**

If a word ends in an **/oa/** sound, the spelling will almost always be **ow**.

Get started

Sort these words into those with a short **/o/** sound (as in **hot**) and words with a long **/oa/** sound (as in **hose**). Put the words into a table like the one below. One has been done for you.

1. gold
2. goat
3. got
4. glow
5. gosh
6. grow
7. gloat
8. groan
9. grown
10. gong

Short **/o/** as in **hot**	Long **/oa/** as in **hose**
	gold

Try these

Copy and complete these words with **oa**, **o–e** or **ow**. One has been done for you.

1.  s t _ n _

    Answer: *stone*

2.  b _ _ t

3.  s n _ _

4.  w i n d _ _

5. 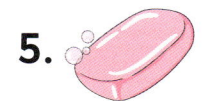 s _ _ p

6.  h _ m _

Now try these

Copy each sentence. Choose the right spelling for the missing word. One has been done for you.

1. The bike zoomed down the _____.
    (sloap / slope / slowp)

    Answer: *The bike zoomed down the slope.*

2. Please _____ me your answer. (shoa / shoe / show)

3. I like _____ ones. (thoas / those / thows)

4. Please don't _____! (moan / mone / mown)

5. Can I _____ your rubber, please? (borroa / borroe / borrow)

6. Whoops! I've burnt the _____! (toast / toste / towst)

Spelling Unit E

Spelling /oo/

The long **/oo/** sound (sometimes said **/yoo/**) can be spelt:

u–e as in J**u**n**e**, t**u**n**e** and fl**u**t**e**

oo as in s**oo**n, m**oo**n and p**oo**l

ue as in bl**ue**, gl**ue** and tiss**ue**

ew as in ph**ew**, n**ew** and gr**ew**

If the **/oo/** sound is at the end of a word, the spelling is often **ue** or **ew**.

Get started

Write these words. Underline the letters in each word that stand for the long **/oo/** or **/yoo/** sound. One has been done for you.

1. June

   Answer: J<u>u</u>n<u>e</u>

2. soon

3. grew

4. tune

5. argue

6. spooky

7. new

8. clue

Try these

Copy and complete these words with **u–e**, **oo**, **ue** or **ew**. One has been done for you.

1. b l _ _

   Answer: blue

2. m _ _ n

3. t _ b _

4. g l _ _

5. f l _ t _

6. b r _ _ m

Now try these

Copy each sentence. Choose the right spelling for the missing word. One has been done for you.

1. Give me a _____. (clue / clew / cloo)

   Answer: Give me a clue.

2. Sunny lost his _____. (tueth / tewth / tooth)

3. Malik is in a bad _____. (mewd / mude / mood)

4. It's _____ – ask Freya! (true / trew / troo)

5. Daisy used Mum's _____. (perfewm / perfume)

6. We need a _____ tube of toothpaste. (nue / new / noo)

Spelling Unit F

Spelling /oi/

The **/oi/** sound can be spelt:

oi as in t**oi**let, j**oi**nt and c**oi**n

–oy as in b**oy**, t**oy** and ann**oy**

The **/oi/** sound is spelt **–oy** at the ends of words. In the middle of a word, **/oi/** is usually spelt **oi** (except for l**oy**al, r**oy**al and v**oy**age).

Get started

Write these words. Underline the letters in each word that stand for the **/oi/** sound. One has been done for you.

1. boil

    Answer: b<u>oi</u>l

2. noise
3. toy
4. royal
5. point
6. boy
7. droid
8. voice

Try these

Copy and complete these words with **oi** or **–oy**. One has been done for you.

1. c _ _ n

    Answer: coin

2. t _ _ s

3. s _ _ l

4. c o w b _ _

5. t _ _ l e t

Now try these

Choose the correct word to complete each sentence. Write the sentences. One has been done for you.

1. Grandpa's dog is very loial / loyal.

    Answer: Grandpa's dog is very loyal.

2. Sophie and I had a joint / joynt birthday party.

3. Mrs Parker has lost her voice / voyce.

4. Did you enjoi / enjoy the film?

5. We planted the seeds in the soil / soyl.

Spelling Unit G

Spelling /ar/

The most common spelling of the long **/ar/** sound is **ar**, as in p**ar**k, l**ar**ge and ch**ar**m.

Get started

Write these words. Underline the letters in each word that stand for the **/ar/** sound. One has been done for you.

1. charm

    Answer: ch<u>ar</u>m
2. cartoon
3. park
4. army
5. garden
6. part
7. hard
8. jar

Try these

Look at each picture and write each word. They all have the /ar/ sound spelt **ar**. One has been done for you.

1. _ _ _ _ _ _

   Answer: carpet

2. _ _ _ _

3. _ _ _ _ _

4. _ _ _ _ _

5. _ _ _ _ _ _

Now try these

Choose the correct word to complete each sentence. Write the sentences. One has been done for you.

| car   scarf   barks   large   start |

1. The dog _____ at night.

   Answer: The dog barks at night.

2. Put on a hat and _____ .

3. A blue whale is very _____ .

4. The film will _____ soon.

5. Carl is parking the _____ .

Spelling Unit H

Spelling the /e/ sound ea

The short **/e/** sound can be spelt **e** as in fr**e**sh, p**e**t and r**e**d.

But it can also be spelt **ea** as in h**ea**d, br**ea**d and h**ea**vy.

Get started

Sort these words into those with a short **/e/** spelt **e** and words with a short **/e/** spelt **ea**. Put the words into a table like the one below. One has been done for you.

1. dread
2. read
3. bet
4. Fred
5. meant
6. sent
7. deaf
8. lend

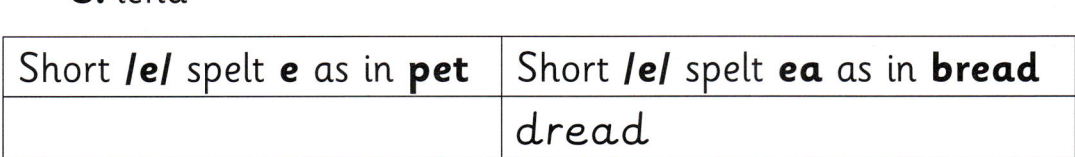

Short **/e/** spelt **e** as in **pet**	Short **/e/** spelt **ea** as in **bread**
	dread

Try these

Look at each picture and write each word. They all have the /e/ sound spelt **ae**. One has been done for you.

1. _ _ _ _ _
   Answer: bread

2. _ _ _ _ _ _ _

3. _ _ _ _ _ _

4. _ _ _ _ _ _

5. _ _ _ _ _

Now try these

Choose the correct word to complete each sentence. Write the sentences. One has been done for you.

| leant   weather   head   ready   heavy |

1. I bumped my _____ on the door.

   Answer: I bumped my head on the door.

2. My school bag is very _____.

3. Mason _____ his bike on the wall.

4. _____, steady, GO!

5. The _____ in Spain is great.

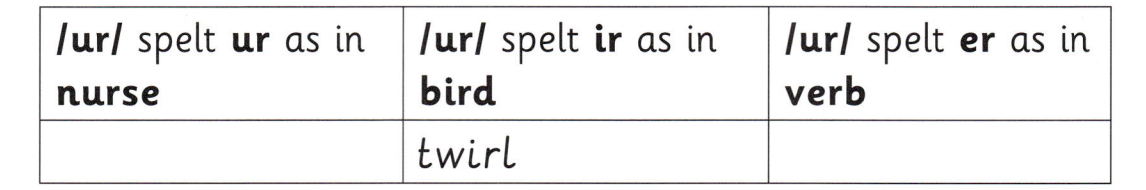

Spelling Unit 1

Spelling /ur/

The long vowel **/ur/** can be spelt:

ur as in n**ur**se, b**ur**st and t**ur**n

ir as in b**ir**d, th**ir**d and b**ir**ch

er as in v**er**b, t**er**m and v**er**se

Get started

Sort these words into **ur**, **ir** and **er** spellings. Put the words into a table like the one below. One has been done for you.

1. twirl
2. curl
3. term
4. shirt
5. person
6. burn
7. dirty
8. burst
9. kerb

/ur/ spelt **ur** as in **nurse**	**/ur/** spelt **ir** as in **bird**	**/ur/** spelt **er** as in **verb**
	twirl	

Try these

Copy and complete each word with **ur**, **ir** or **er**. One has been done for you.

1. f _ _ s t

   Answer: first

2. s k _ _ t

3. n _ _ s e

4. p _ _ p l e

5. h _ _ b s

Now try these

Choose the correct word to complete each sentence. Write the sentences. One has been done for you.

| person   hurting   curly   birthday   chirps |

1. Ali has _____ hair.

   Answer: Ali has curly hair.

2. My head is really _____.

3. It is my _____ on Sunday.

4. The bird _____ on the branch.

5. I am the youngest _____ in my family.

Spelling Unit J

Spelling the short /oo/

The short **/oo/** sound can be spelt:

oo as in b**oo**k, l**oo**k and c**oo**k

u as in p**u**sh, b**u**sh and p**u**dding

The most common spelling is **oo**.

Get started

Sort these words into those with the short **/oo/** sound spelt **u** (as in **full**) and words with the short **/oo/** sound spelt **oo** (as in **foot**). Put the words into a table like the one below. One has been done for you.

1. good
2. push
3. cook
4. put
5. brook
6. look
7. pull
8. rook

Short **/oo/** spelt **u** as in **full**	Short **/oo/** spelt **oo** as in **foot**
	good

Try these

Choose the correct spelling. Write the word. One has been done for you.

1. foot / fut

   Answer: foot

2. wood / wud

3. boosh / bush

4. hook / huk

5. pooding / pudding

Now try these

Choose the correct word to complete each sentence. Write the sentences. One has been done for you.

| book   stood   good   wool   cooking |

1. The sheep had thick _____.

   Answer: The sheep had thick wool.

2. The play last night was really _____.

3. Amber is reading a good _____.

4. Cavan and his dad enjoy _____.

5. We _____ up to sing.

Spelling Unit K

Spelling /or/

The **/or/** sound can be spelt:

or as in h**or**se, sh**or**t and h**or**n

aw as in **aw**ful, dr**aw** and cl**aw**

ore as in m**ore**, st**ore** and sh**ore**

au as in p**au**se, s**au**ce and **au**thor

If the **/or/** sound is at the end of a word, the spelling is likely to be **–aw** or **–ore**.

Get started

Write these words. Underline the letters in each word that stand for the **/or/** sound. One has been done for you.

1. author
   Answer: a<u>u</u>thor
2. paw
3. astronaut
4. yawn
5. daub
6. more
7. dinosaur
8. August

Try these

Choose the correct spelling. Write the word. One has been done for you.

1. crawl / crorl

    Answer: crawl

2. bawn / born
3. mawning / morning
4. lawn / lorn
5. spawt / sport

Now try these

Choose the correct word to complete each sentence. Write the sentence. One has been done for you.

| horses | wore | before | anymore | explore |

1. I don't sit by Jim _____.

    Answer: I don't sit by Jim anymore.

2. Stella _____ her new shoes.
3. Have you been ice-skating _____?
4. I like to ride _____.
5. Let's _____ the castle!

Review unit 1

Can you remember the spellings you've learned this term? Answer these questions to find out.

A. Can you find the words that rhyme? Write these words as rhyming pairs.

bone   train   sheet   foam   shine   kite

home   meat   fright   plane   sign   grown

B. Look at each picture. Write the word.

1.    sh _ _ _

2.    b _ _ _ _

3.    sh _ _ _

4.    fish h _ _ _

5.    tomato s _ _ _ _

6.    lion's p _ _

26

C. Underline the word in each sentence that is spelt incorrectly.

1. That was a gud book.
2. My chare is wobbly.
3. Tim came ferst in the race.
4. My dad has a shiny hed.
5. Can I joyn your game?
6. The beanstalk grue up to the sky.

Spelling Unit L

Spelling /ou/

The **/ou/** sound can be spelt:

ow as in h**ow**, n**ow** and c**ow**

ou as in **ou**t, l**ou**d and m**ou**se

Get started

Write these words. Underline the letters in each word that stand for the **/ou/** sound. One has been done for you.

1. found

    Answer: f<u>ou</u>nd

2. drown
3. count
4. howl
5. sound
6. brown
7. south
8. town

Try these

Copy and complete these words with **ou** or **ow**. One has been done for you.

1. m _ _ t h

   Answer: mouth

2. c _ _

3. m _ _ s e

4. c r _ _ n

5. c l _ _ n

Now try these

Choose the correct word to complete each sentence. Write the sentences. One has been done for you.

1. Mix the _____, milk and eggs.   (flowr / flour)

   Answer: Mix the flour, milk and eggs.

2. Joseph got lost in the _____.   (crowd / croud)

3. I have _____ eyes.   (brown / broun)

4. Run _____ the playground!   (arownd / around)

5. Billy and Max _____ the bricks.   (cownt / count)

Spelling Unit M

Spelling /air/

The **/air/** sound can be spelt:

air as in f**air**, h**air** and ch**air**

are as in sp**are**, c**are** and prep**are**

ear as in p**ear**, b**ear** and w**ear**

Get started

Write these words. Underline the letters in each word that stand for the **/air/** sound. One has been done for you.

1. pear

    Answer: p<u>ear</u>

2. flair
3. share
4. pair
5. hare
6. bear
7. stair
8. blare

Try these

Choose the correct spelling. Write the word. One has been done for you.

1. tear / tare / tair

    Answer: tear

2. chear / chare / chair

3. feary / farey / fairy

4. cear / care / cair

5. deary / darey / dairy

Now try these

Write these sentences. Underline the words that have the **/air/** sound. One has been done for you.

1. I am scared of bears.

    Answer: I am <u>scared</u> of <u>bears</u>.

2. It's not fair if you don't share with me.

3. Don't wear that dress — it has a tear in it.

4. Please can you share that pear with me.

5. I'm going upstairs to get a pair of slippers.

Spelling Unit N

Spelling /ear/

The **/ear/** sound can be spelt:

ear as in n**ear**, f**ear** and cl**ear**

ere as in h**ere** and sph**ere**

eer as in ch**eer**, sn**eer** and p**eer**

Most words with this sound are spelt **ear**.

Get started

Write the words from this list that have the **/ear/** sound.

1. clear
2. near
3. fear
4. where
5. were
6. here
7. bear

Try these

Choose the correct spelling. Write the word. One has been done for you.

1. year / yere

   Answer: year

2. clear / clere

3. snear / sneer

4. hear / heer

5. fear / fere

Now try these

Choose the correct word to complete each sentence. Write the sentence. One has been done for you.

> beard   dear   deer   clearly   cheer

1. Can you try to _____ up your sister?

   Answer: Can you try to cheer up your sister?

2. _____ Granny,

   Thank you for my present.

3. Uncle Dave has grown a _____.

4. A baby _____ is called a fawn.

5. Speak loudly and _____, please.

Spelling Unit 1

Spelling –ff, –ll, –ss and –zz

Many words have double letters at the end (**–ff**, **–ll**, **–ss** and **–zz**). We use double letters at the ends of short words with short vowel sounds.
For example: o**ff**, we**ll**, mi**ss** and bu**zz**

Get started

Copy these words and underline the double letters (**–ll**, **–ff**, **–ss** or **–zz**) at the end of each word. One has been done for you.

1. shell

    Answer: she*ll*

2. fuss
3. off
4. press
5. ill
6. troll
7. glass
8. cliff

Try these

Choose and copy the correct spelling of each word. One has been done for you.

1. dol / doll

    Answer: doll

2. smell / smel

3. buz / buzz

4. fluff / fluf

5. mess / mes

Now try these

Copy these sentences adding **–ll** or **–ss** to the ends of the words to finish them. One has been done for you.

1. Jill has a do_ _.

    Answer: Jill has a doll.

2. Ring the doorbe_ _.

3. Cut the gra_ _.

4. Do not mi_ _ the bus.

5. Roll down the hi_ _.

Spelling Unit 2

Spelling –ck after a short vowel

When a word ends with a **/k/** sound and it has a short vowel sound in the middle, it is spelt **–ck**. For example: ba**ck**

Get started

Copy these words and underline **–ck** at the end of each word. One has been done for you.

1. shock

    Answer: sho<u>ck</u>

2. tick
3. lick
4. rock
5. luck

Try these

Look at each picture and write each word (they all end **–ck**).
One has been done for you.

1.  a ba<u>ck</u>pa<u>ck</u>

2.  a t_ _ _ _

3.  a b_ _ _ _ dog

4.  a s_ _ _ _ of b_ _ _ _s

Now try these

Copy and complete the sentences with words from the list.
One has been done for you.

| quack | black | brick | clock | trick |

1. The duck went _____.

   Answer: The duck went quack.

2. The _____ wall is very high.

3. The cat is _____.

4. The dog did a _____.

5. The _____ tells the time.

Spelling Unit 3

Spelling −nk

The **/ng−k/** sound is spelt **−nk**.
For example: ba**nk**, thi**nk**, ho**nk** and sku**nk**

Get started

Copy these words and underline **−nk** at the end of each word. One has been done for you.

1. drink

    Answer: dri<u>nk</u>

2. pink
3. plank
4. ink
5. sunk
6. clunk
7. think
8. blank

Try these

Choose and copy the correct spelling of each word. One has been done for you.

1. stink / stinc

    Answer: stink

2. bunk / bunc

3. junc / junk

4. blink / blinc

5. banc / bank

Now try these

Copy and complete the sentences with words from the list. One has been done for you.

| trunk   thank   sink   bunk   wink |

1. The elephant has a long _____.

    Answer: The elephant has a long trunk.

2. Wash your hands in the _____.

3. It is polite to say _____ you.

4. Closing one eye is called a _____.

5. My brother and I sleep on _____ beds.

Spelling Unit 4

Spelling words with two syllables

Long words can be split into parts called syllables. Syllables are like beats. For example, the word **sunset** has two syllables (beats): **sun / set**. It is easier to spell long words if you split them into their syllables.

Get started

Sort these words into two groups: words that have one syllable and words that have two syllables. Put them into a table like the one below. One has been done for you.

1. frog
2. carrot
3. bed
4. chicken
5. pocket

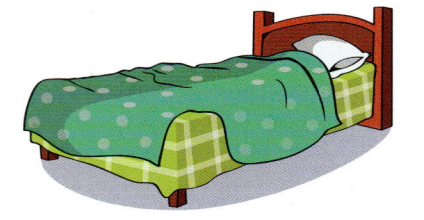

One syllable	Two syllables
frog	

Try these

Look at each picture and write the words. They all have two syllables. One has been done for you.

1.  s _ _ _ _ _ _ _

2. k _ _ _ _ _

Answer: s e a h o r s e

3.  z _ _ _ _

4.  p _ _ _ _ _

5. h _ _ _ _ _ _

Now try these

Copy each sentence and underline the words that have two syllables in each sentence. One has been done for you.

1. The spotty dog has two puppies.

    Answer: The <u>spotty</u> dog has two <u>puppies</u>.

2. I wear my jumper to keep warm.

3. I eat bread and butter.

4. I saw monkeys at the zoo.

5. Daisies are white and yellow flowers.

Spelling Unit 5

Spelling the /ch/ sound tch

The **/ch/** sound is spelt **tch** if it comes straight after a short vowel.
For example: ca**tch**

Get started

Copy and complete these words and underline **tch** in each word. One has been done for you.

1. catch
   Answer: ca<u>tch</u>
2. pitch
3. crutch
4. snatch
5. latch
6. hatch
7. wa_ _ _
8. ke_ _ _up
9. ske_ _ _
10. ki_ _ _en

42

Try these

Find the misspelt words in these sentences where the **/ch/** sound should be spelt **tch**. Write out the sentences with the correct spelling. One has been done for you.

1. My dog feches sticks.

    Answer: My dog fetches sticks.

2. My rabbit lives in a huch.
3. I like to wach television.
4. The pirate has an eye pach.
5. Measles make you ich and scrach.

Now try these

Sort these words into two groups: words spelt **–tch** and words spelt **–ch**.

- much
- notch
- which
- stretch
- switch
- chin

Spelt –tch	Spelt –ch

Spelling Unit 6

Spelling words that end in a /v/ sound

Words that end with a **/v/** sound are spelt **–ve**.
For example: glo**ve**

Get started

Copy these words and underline **–ve** in each word. One has been done for you.

1. glove

    Answer: glo<u>ve</u>

2. captive
3. dissolve
4. olive
5. serve
6. have
7. remove
8. move
9. wave

Try these

Put the letters in the correct order to spell each word. One has been done for you.

carve	curve	starve
love	solve	

1. acrev

   Answer: carve

2. ovel

3. rastev

4. vecur

5. oslev

Now try these

Write these sentences and underline the words that end in **–ve** in the sentences. One has been done for you.

1. On birthdays, people give presents.

   Answer: On birthdays, people <u>give</u> presents.

2. It is good to be active.

3. I have a pet dove.

4. Blue whales are massive!

5. I live in a flat above a shop.

Spelling Unit 7

Adding –s

For most nouns, you add an **–s** to make a plural (to show there's more than one).
For example: one rabbit, two rabbit**s**

Sometimes you need to add an **–s** to a verb if someone else is performing the action.
For example: I lick a lolly, he lick**s** a lolly

Get started

For each noun, decide whether to add an **–s** or not. Write the phrase. One has been done for you.

1. two rabbit

    Answer: two rabbits

2. a banana
3. many hand
4. one log
5. one hundred book

Try these

Choose the correct word to complete each phrase. Write the phrase. One has been done for you.

1. he drink / drinks

    Answer: he drinks

2. I run / runs
3. she hop / hops
4. you rock / rocks
5. it suck / sucks

Now try these

Choose the correct word to complete each sentence. Write the sentence. One has been done for you.

1. The chicken / chickens has laid two egg / eggs.

    Answer: The chicken has laid two eggs.

2. I can see two cow / cows in the field.
3. Rashid kick / kicks the ball.
4. Harriet eat / eats a lot of fresh fruit.
5. I have two pen / pens and one pencil / pencils.

Spelling Unit 8

Adding –es to make a plural

Sometimes you need to add **–es** to a noun to make it a plural (to show there is more than one).
For example: one fox, two fox**es**

The same is true for verbs. Sometimes you need to add **–es** to a verb if someone else is performing the action.
For example: I wish, she wish**es**

Adding **–es** to a word adds another syllable.

Get started

For each noun, decide whether to add **–es** or not. Write the phrase. One has been done for you.

1. a fox

    Answer: a fox

2. some dish
3. three wish
4. lots of match
5. one cross

Try these

Choose the correct word to complete each phrase. Write the phrase. One has been done for you.

1. Tim brush / brushes.

    Answer: Tim brushes.

2. I fetch / fetches.
3. It switch / switches.
4. We watch / watches.
5. She catch / catches.

Now try these

Choose the correct spelling to complete each sentence. Write the sentence. One has been done for you.

1. My hat matchs / matches my gloves!

    Answer: My hat matches my gloves!

2. My brother plays / playes the piano.
3. My dog bites / bitees and scratchs / scratches.
4. Henri reads / reades a lot of books / bookes.
5. My aunt gives me lots of hugs / hugges and kisss / kisses.

Review unit 2

Can you remember the spellings you've learned this term? Answer these questions to find out.

A. Look at each picture and write each word.

1.  s h _ _ _
2.  r _ _ _
3.  s k _ _ _
4.  d _ _ _
5.  d r _ _ _
6.  d _ _ _
7.  s _ _ _
8.  c r _ _ _
9.  t r _ _ _

50

B. Can you write these two-syllable words? Look at the pictures and write the words. They all have two syllables. Watch out, some of them are plurals!

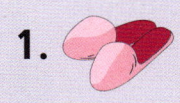

1. s l _ _ _ _ _ _
2. h _ _ _ _ _
3. c r _ _ _ _ _ _
4. d _ _ _ _ _ _
5. t _ _ _ _
6. f _ _ _ _ _
   c _ _ _ _ _

C. Copy and complete the sentences. Choose the correct spellings for the missing words.

1. Where is your other _____? (glov / glove)
2. I like _____ on my chips. (ketchup / kechup)
3. Press the light _____ to turn the light on. (swich / switch)
4. Can I _____ the TV, please? (wach / watch)
5. _____ me a seat. (save / sav)
6. I have a new _____ of shoes. (pear / pair)

Spelling Unit 9

Adding –ing to a root word

To add **–ing** to most words you do not need to change the root word at all. Just add **–ing**.
For example: sleep + **–ing** → sleep**ing**

Adding **–ing** to a word adds another syllable.

Get started

Add **–ing** to the end of each word. One has been done for you.

1. sleep

    Answer: sleeping

2. dress
3. buzz
4. fizz
5. hunt
6. clean
7. jump
8. eat

Try these

Copy the two lists and match the words that end with **–ing** with their root words. One has been done for you.

–ing words	root words
blinking	dry
sinking	lick
licking	blink
snowing	sink
drying	snow

Now try these

There should be a word that ends with **–ing** in each of these sentences. For each sentence, work out which word needs **–ing** and then copy the sentence, adding **–ing** where it's needed. One has been done for you.

1. We are play with the toys.

    Answer: We are playing with the toys.

2. The eggs are hatch.

3. We are watch the school play.

4. Mena is kick the ball.

5. Outside it is rain.

Spelling Unit 10

Adding –er to a root word

To add **–er** to most words you do not need to change the root word at all. Just add **–er**.
For example: jump + **–er** → jump**er**

Adding **–er** to a word adds another syllable.

Get started

Add **–er** to the end of each word. One has been done for you.

1. row

    Answer: rower

2. hunt
3. print
4. read
5. think
6. clean
7. sweep
8. cook

54

Try these

Copy the two lists and match the words that end with **–er** with their root words. One has been done for you.

–er words	root words
singer	mix
helper	work
worker	sing
caller	help
mixer	call

Now try these

There should be a word that ends with **–er** in each of these sentences. For each sentence, work out which word needs **–er** and then copy the sentence, adding **–er** where it's needed. One has been done for you.

1. Jose is a fantastic football play.

    Answer: Jose is a fantastic football <u>player</u>.

2. The garden cut the grass.

3. The build is building a house.

4. Mrs Brown is my teach.

5. Billy has always been a dream.

Spelling Unit 11

Adding –ed to a root word

To add **–ed** to many words you do not need to change the root word at all. Just add **–ed**.
For example: enjoy + **–ed** → enjoy**ed**

Sometimes adding **–ed** to a word adds another syllable. For example, hunted. Sometimes the **e** doesn't stand for a sound so the **–ed** just stands for **/d/**, for example, enjoy**ed**.

Get started

Copy these words. Add **–ed** to the end of each word. One has been done for you.

1. dress

    Answer: dressed

2. fizz
3. play
4. sort
5. snow
6. cook

Try these

Copy the two lists and match the words that end with **–ed** with their root words. One has been done for you.

–ed words	**root words**
kicked	park
parked	blink
itched	kick
blinked	pull
pulled	itch

Now try these

There should be a word that ends with **–ed** in each of these sentences. For each sentence, work out which word needs **–ed** and then copy the sentence, adding **–ed** where it's needed. One has been done for you.

1. Joel paint a picture.

    Answer: *Joel painted a picture.*

2. Last night, it snow.
3. The dog pant in the heat.
4. Jack clean his bedroom.
5. Dad cook dinner last night.

Spelling Unit 12

Adding –er and –est to adjectives

If you want to compare things, add **–er** to the end of an adjective. If you want to describe something as the 'most' of anything, add **–est** to the end of an adjective. Many adjectives do not change when **–er** or **–est** is added to them. Both endings always add another syllable to the word.
For example: small, small**er**, small**est**

Get started

Copy these words and underline **–er** or **–est** at the end of each word. One has been done for you.

1. small   smaller   smallest
   Answer: small   small<u>er</u>   small<u>est</u>
2. kind   kinder   kindest
3. cold   colder   coldest
4. clean   cleaner   cleanest
5. pink   pinker   pinkest
6. dark   darker   darkest
7. neat   neater   neatest

Try these

Put the letters in the correct order to spell each word. They all end in **–er** or **–est**. One has been done for you.

greener	fuller	nearest
faster	longest	

1. erergne
2. oestlgn

   Answer: greener

3. srtfae
4. esarnet
5. ulefrl

Now try these

Add **–er** or **–est** to the end of the unfinished word or words in each sentence. One has been done for you.

1. Giraffes are the tall_____ animals on Earth.

   Answer: Giraffes are the tall<u>est</u> animals on Earth.

2. Feathers are soft_____ than stones.
3. Africa is warm_____ than Iceland.
4. My dad is the short_____ man I know.
5. My brother is strong. I am even strong_____. But my mum is the strong_____.

59

Spelling Unit 13

Spelling words ending in –y

The **/ee/** at the end of a word is often spelt **–y**.
For example: tast**y**

Get started

Copy these words and underline the **–y** at the end of each word. One has been done for you.

1. tasty

    Answer: tasty
2. party
3. family
4. hurry
5. bendy
6. fizzy
7. messy
8. angry
9. yummy

Try these

Write the correct spelling of each word. One has been done for you.

1. crazee / crazy

    Answer: crazy

2. lucky / luckie
3. jolly / jolli
4. mucki / mucky
5. crunchy / crunche

Now try these

Find the misspelt words in these sentences. Write the sentences using the correct spellings. One has been done for you.

1. The sillee clown fell over his big shoes.

    Answer: The silly clown fell over his big shoes.

2. I went on a scari ride at the fair.
3. Josh felt sleepie after swimming.
4. It was a veri windie day.
5. I ride my ponie everi day.

Spelling Unit 14

Spelling ph

Sometimes the **/f/** sound is spelt **ph**.
For example: dol**ph**in, ele**ph**ant

Get started

Copy these words and underline the **ph** in each word. One has been done for you.

1. dolphin

    Answer: dol<u>ph</u>in

2. phantom
3. phonics
4. telegraph
5. microphone
6. elephant
7. graph
8. photograph
9. nephew

62

Try these

Put the letters in the correct order to spell each word. They all have the /f/ sound spelt **ph**. One has been done for you.

~~phrase~~	microphone	orphan
telephone	graph	

1. hespar

    Answer: phrase

2. oetleepnh

3. onepimcroh

4. grhap

5. panhor

Now try these

Find the misspelt word in each sentence. Write the sentences with the correct spellings. One has been done for you.

1. Elefants are very big animals.

    Answer: Elephants are very big animals.

2. I can say the alfabet backwards.

3. My mother's nefew is my cousin.

4. Megafones make your voice louder.

5. Make a fotocopy of this page.

Spelling Unit 15

Spelling wh

Sometimes the /w/ sound is spelt **wh–**. For example: **wh**ale. Some of these are question words:
what, **wh**ere, **wh**en, **wh**ich and **wh**y.

Get started

Copy these words and underline the **wh–** in each word. One has been done for you.

1. whale

    Answer: <u>wh</u>ale

2. what
3. where
4. wheel
5. whisper
6. wheeze
7. whine
8. white
9. why

Try these

Put the letters in the correct order to spell each word. They all start with **wh–**. One has been done for you.

| ~~whisk~~ | why | white | when | which |

1. hikws

   Answer: *whisk*

2. nhew

3. chhiw

4. thewi

5. hyw

Now try these

Find the misspelt word in each sentence. Write the sentences with the correct spellings. One has been done for you.

1. I keep a wite rabbit as a pet.

   Answer: *I keep a white rabbit as a pet.*

2. I wonder wy the sky is blue.

3. Wen will it be your birthday?

4. Please tell me wat your name is.

5. I use a weelchair to get around.

Spelling Unit 16

Spelling words with k

The **/k/** sound is usually spelt **k** (instead of **c**) if it is before **e**, **i** or **y**.
For example: **k**itten

The letter **k** also stands for the **/k/** sound when it is with a long vowel.
For example: bi**k**e

Get started

Copy these words and underline the long vowel and letter **k** in each word. One has been done for you.

1. bike

   Answer: bike

2. strike
3. stroke
4. bake
5. fake
6. broke
7. hike

66

Try these

Sort these words into three groups: words where **k** comes before **e**, before **i** and before **y**. Put the words into a table like the one below. One has been done for you.

1. kettle
2. skin
3. frisky
4. kid
5. kennel

k before e	k before i	k before y
kettle		

Now try these

Copy and complete the sentences with words from the list. One has been done for you.

kite   king   kitchen   cakes   stinky   sky

1. I like to fly my ____ on windy days.
   Answer: I like to fly my kite on windy days.
2. Dirty socks smell _____.
3. I like watching clouds in the _____.
4. The _____ rules over this land.
5. I like to bake _____ in the _____.

67

Spelling Unit 17

Adding the prefix un–

When the letters **un** (called the prefix **un–**) are added to a word they change its meaning to the opposite of what it meant before. For example: to be kind means to be nice, but to be **un**kind is to be horrible. When you add **un–**, the root word does not need to change.
For example: **un–** + kind → **un**kind

Get started

Add **un–** to the beginning of each word. One has been done for you.

1. __wrap

    Answer: <u>un</u>wrap

2. __zip
3. __lucky
4. __do
5. __safe
6. __plug
7. __lock

Try these

Match each word with its meaning, by choosing one of these words to copy. One has been done for you.

| unafraid | unfair | unhappy | unpack | untidy |

1. brave

    Answer: unafraid

2. messy

3. not fair

4. take out

5. sad

Now try these

There should be a word beginning with **un–** in each of these sentences. For each sentence, work out which word needs **un–** and then copy the sentence, adding **un–** where it's needed. One has been done for you.

1. Tommy dressed before having a bath.

    Answer: Tommy <u>un</u>dressed before having a bath.

2. To open the door you must lock it first.
3. The sink is blocked. We need to plug it.
4. That nasty boy is very kind.
5. My muddy boots are very clean.

Spelling Unit 18

Spelling compound words

Compound words are two words joined together to make a new word. The spellings of the two original words stay the same.
For example: **handbag**

Get started

Split these compound words into two words. One has been done for you.

1. football
   Answer: *foot   ball*
2. bedroom
3. blackberry
4. popcorn
5. afternoon
6. sunflower
7. snowman
8. goldfish

Try these

Choose words from the box to make compound words. One has been done for you.

~~mother~~ yard shine storm fish ~~grand~~

1. grand   Answer: grandmother
2. thunder
3. star
4. farm
5. sun

Now try these

Write the missing word for each sentence. One has been done for you.

jellyfish footprints bookmark airport hairbrush

1. I do not want to be stung by a _____.

   Answer: I do not want to be stung by a jellyfish.

2. Tilly brushed her hair with a _____.
3. We took a bus to the _____.
4. Our feet left _____ in the sand.
5. I put a _____ in my book.

Spelling Unit 19

Spelling the days of the week

Practise spelling the days of the week. Each word ends with **day** but some of the words have special spellings you need to remember.

Sunday	Sun / day	
Monday	Mon / day	(The **/u/** sound is spelt **o**)
Tuesday	Tues / day	(The long **/oo/** sound is spelt **ue**)
Wednesday	Wed / nes / day	(The **d** and the second **e** are 'silent')
Thursday	Thurs / day	(The **/er/** sound is spelt **ur**)
Friday	Fri / day	(The long **/igh/** sound is spelt **i**)
Saturday	Sat / ur / day	(The **/er/** sound is spelt **ur**)

Remember, each one starts with a capital letter.

Get started

Copy the days of the week. Underline the capital letters at the beginning and **day** at the end of each one. One has been done for you.

1. Sunday   Answer: <u>S</u>un<u>day</u>   2. Monday
3. Tuesday   4. Wednesday   5. Thursday
6. Friday   7. Saturday

Try these

Add the missing letters to complete each word. One has been done for you.

1. S _ _ day

    Answer: Sunday

2. M _ _ day

3. T_ _ _ day

4. W_ _ _ _ _ day

5. T_ _ _ _ day

6. F_ _ day

7. S_ _ _ _ day

Now try these

Copy and complete each sentence with the days of the week. One has been done for you.

1. On Su _ _ _ _, we fed the ducks.

    Answer: On Sunday, we fed the ducks.

2. M _ _ _ _ _ is the first day of the school week.

3. On Tu _ _ _ _ _, Saul goes to karate.

4. Seb swims on W _ _ _ _ _ _ _ _.

5. Granny is visiting on Th _ _ _ _ _ _.

6. We are going on holiday on F _ _ _ _ _.

7. Let's go to town on Sa _ _ _ _ _ _.

Spelling Unit 20

Spelling common exception words

Many of the words we use every day have spellings that don't follow the rules we've learned. For example, some words spell the **/z/** sound **s**, such as i**s**, hi**s**, say**s**, wa**s** and ha**s**; some words use the letters **ere** to spell different sounds, such as h**ere**, wh**ere**, th**ere** and w**ere**. They all need to be learned. Practise spelling these tricky words.

Get started

Write out each word three times. Underline the part that isn't spelt the way it's said. One has been done for you.

1. today

    Answer: t<u>o</u>day t<u>o</u>day t<u>o</u>day

2. of
3. said
4. they
5. come
6. some
7. friend
8. school

Try these

Write the correct spelling of each word. One has been done for you.

1. hiz / his

    Answer: his

2. was / waz
3. is / iz
4. sayz / says
5. has / haz

Now try these

Copy and complete the sentences with words from the list. One has been done for you.

| were | where | here | once | there | are | our |

1. _____ is Jess?
2. _____ you nearly ready yet?
3. Come _____ now!
4. This is _____ house.
5. _____ upon a time _____ _____ three bears.

Review unit 3

Can you remember the spellings you've learned this term? Answer these questions to find out.

A. Look at each picture and write the word.

1. b _ _ _

2. e _ _ _ _ _ _ _

3. r _ _ _ _ _ _

4. w _ _ _ _

5. d _ _ _ _ _ _

6. f _ _ _ _ _ _ _ s

7. s _ _ _ _

B. Add the beginning or ending to each word. Write the new words.

1. read + ing
2. clean + er
3. look + ed
4. tall + est
5. say + ing
6. un + happy

C. Find the misspelt words in each sentence. Write each sentence using the correct spelling.

1. Wen will dinner be ready?
2. Wair are your shoes?
3. Wi is the sky blue?
4. Please put the cettle on.
5. I play tennis on Whensdays.
6. Tara is my best frend.
7. Here thay are!
8. Can I have sume cake?